MAD
Science

KITCHEN SCIENCE EXPERIMENTS

How Does Your Mold Garden Grow?

By Sudipta Bardhan-Quallen

Illustrated by Edward Miller

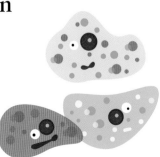

STERLING

New York / London
www.sterlingpublishing.com/kids

STERLING and the distinctive Sterling logo are registered trademarks of Sterling Publishing Co., Inc.

Library of Congress Cataloging-in-Publication Data
Bardhan-Quallen, Sudipta.
Kitchen science experiments : how does your mold garden grow? /
by Sudipta Brdhan-Quallen ; illustrated by Eward Miller.
p. cm. — (Mad science)
Includes bibliographical references and index.
ISBN 978-1-4027-2413-8 (hc-plc with jacket : alk. paper)
1. Microbiology—Experiments—Juvenile literature.
2. Biology—Experiments—Juvenile literature.
I. Miller, Edward, 1964- ill. II. Title.
QR57.B37 2010
579—dc22
2010003749

Lot #:
2 4 6 8 10 9 7 5 3 1
08/10
Published by Sterling Publishing Co., Inc.
387 Park Avenue South, New York, NY 10016
© 2010 by Sudipta Bardhan-Quallen
Illustrations © 2010 by Edward Miller
Distributed in Canada by Sterling Publishing
^c/o Canadian Manda Group, 165 Dufferin Street
Toronto, Ontario, Canada M6K 3H6
Distributed in the United Kingdom by GMC Distribution Services
Castle Place, 166 High Street, Lewes, East Sussex, England BN7 1XU
Distributed in Australia by Capricorn Link (Australia) Pty. Ltd.
P.O. Box 704, Windsor, NSW 2756, Australia

Printed in China
All rights reserved.

Sterling ISBN 978-1-4027-2413-8

For information about custom editions, special sales, premium and
corporate purchases, please contact Sterling Special Sales
Department at 800-805-5489 or specialsales@sterlingpublishing.com.

Designed by Edward Miller

Contents

Introduction

How to Be a Mad Scientist in Eight Easy Steps

1. ASK QUESTIONS. Scientific research is about answering questions—so the first step is to have them. All scientists start by questioning the world around them. (How did this banana get all black and greasy? Why do some things fizz when I mix them while other things change color? Is there anything alive in my belly button?) The topics and projects in this book will give you a starting point, but don't be afraid to go beyond them and design your own experiments.

2. KEEP YOUR EYES PEELED. You can never know where your next mad inspiration will come from, so examine everything you see. Does the tree outside seem to be growing at an odd angle? Does Monday's leftover lunch seem to be rotting in your locker more quickly than usual? Since your parents changed laundry detergent, do your gym clothes stay fresher for a longer time? By observing the world, you will uncover great ideas that you can add to the experiments in this book and discover ideas for new projects.

3. BE PREPARED FOR ANYTHING. True mad scientists are always ready to dive right into their work. But a good tip is to carry a notebook and pencil at all times to record anything unusual you might see or any experiment ideas you might have. Other things to keep handy are a magnifying glass to get up close and personal with potential experiments, tweezers to handle small or potentially icky things, and zippered baggies to collect samples (such as moldy food or dead fish). Don't fear the yucky.

4. BE INFORMED. You might want to do some background reading and research to fully appreciate the experiments in this book. Search the Internet or your local library for useful information. By learning what people already know about a subject, you'll be able to do more valuable scientific experiments and uncover new things.

5. TAKE A FEW SUGGESTIONS. Expert scientists go to meetings where they can talk about their experiments—you should do the same. Talk to your friends, parents, and teachers about the experiments that you are doing. They might have good suggestions or ideas about different things you could try.

6. GET A HENCHMAN. A lot of experiments will require help, so enlist a friend or an adult (if there are any safety concerns) to make things go smoothly.

7. BE CAREFUL. The most important thing during any scientific experiment is that you live to experiment again! Follow directions and use care around chemicals—even the household variety—and things such as knives or ovens. Learn how to use your tools correctly.

SAFETY FIRST

8. HAVE FUN! You know how to do that, right?

Chapter 1
It's Alive!

Look around your kitchen. What do the glass of milk on the counter, the sponge in the sink, and the stuff in the fruit bowl all have in common? THEY'RE ALIVE!!!! Well, for the most part, there are critters on or in these things that are very much alive. Yes, it's true, your kitchen is a veritable jungle of life. And life starts with the cell.

Cells, cells, cells

A bacterium is one. So is an amoeba. A microscopic adult worm called *Caenorhabditis elegans* has around 959 of them in its body. Even you have them—in fact, you are made up of more than one hundred trillion of them. What are we talking about? Cells, of course!

Every living organism in the world is made of cells, the teeny-tiny building blocks of life which come in all shapes and varieties (actually, cells have even teenier-tinier parts, but we'll get to that later). Although living organisms are very diverse, cells are not.

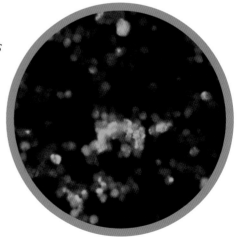

In this photograph, cells have been magnified and stained with fluorescent dye so that they are easier to see.

There are a number of basic parts common to all cells. These include a nucleus, a nuclear membrane, a cell membrane, the cytoplasm, and some mitochondria.

Cells are usually transparent when viewed through a microscope, but scientists have developed different dyes called stains to make viewing cells easier. Some of these stains color only certain types of cells; other stains color only certain parts of cells.

Microscope tips

Some of you mad scientists have had a lot of microscope experience, but it's always a good idea to refresh your knowledge.

- Make sure the microscope is clean before you use it. Use only lens paper to clean the lenses (also called "objectives"). You can find lens paper at science supply stores or your local eyeglass shop.
- Always begin with the microscope stage lowered and with the lowest-powered lens in place. Put the slide carefully on the microscope stage and, using the stage clips, secure it in place.
- To focus the image on the slide, first lower the stage using the coarse focus dial. Do not raise the stage too fast when you are using the coarse focus dial, because the lens could crash into the slide and damage both.
- When you get to the higher-powered lenses, use only the fine focus knob to adjust the image. If you totally lose focus, return to a lower-powered objective and start again.

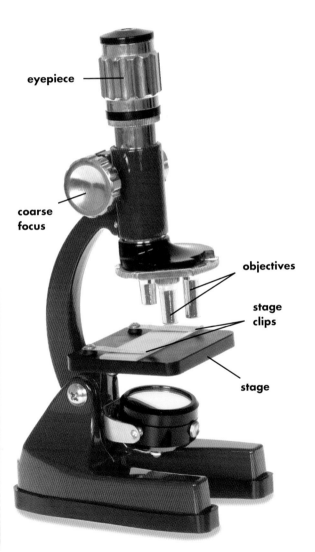

eyepiece

coarse focus

objectives

stage clips

stage

EXPERIMENT: Color a cell

Define a cell in color.

MATERIALS
- microscope
- microscope slides
- cover slips
- iodine
- eyedropper
- pair of tweezers
- one onion

STEP 1: COLLECT THE CELLS.
Use the tweezers to carefully lift off a thin layer of onion skin (don't use the dried outer skin; instead, aim to grab the transparent skin off the moist part of the onion). Lay the onion skin gently on a microscope slide, trying to keep it as flat as possible. Use the eyedropper to place a drop of water on the slide over the onion skin. Carefully place a cover slip over the water and thin onion skin.

STEP 2: : COLOR AND VIEW.
Place a small drop of iodine on one corner of the cover slip. It will spread over the onion skin underneath. Place the slide under the microscope and examine it at different magnifications. What can you see? Draw a picture. Can you identify the different cellular structures on your drawing by comparing it to the cell diagram on the next page? Can you see anything moving inside the cells?

EXTENSION ACTIVITY: Repeat this experiment using other types of samples such as paper-thin slices of potato or cork. What similarities and differences do you notice between the different types of cells? You could also try this experiment using stains other than iodine, such as food color, grape juice, or fabric dyes. Do different cell structures get colored by the different stains?

Be careful when handling chemicals such as iodine. Direct contact with iodine can irritate your skin or eyes.

What's going on?

The nucleus is usually one of the largest structures inside the cell. It is the "control center" of the cell, responsible for telling the cell what to do. The nuclear membrane separates the nucleus from the rest of the cell, just as the cell membrane separates the cell from the outside environment and other cells. Both membranes function as walls and keep the substances within their borders from spilling out. The cytoplasm is the watery material that fills the inside of the cell. The mitochondria are the structures that make energy for the cell.

Plant cells, like the onion you observed in iodine solution, are different from animal cells because they have a few extra parts. They have an outer rigid structure called a cell wall, and chloroplasts, which are small structures that hold chlorophyll, a green pigment that plants use to make energy. Having strong cell walls allows trees to become the tallest living things on earth, and makes wood such a great construction material.

Plant Cell

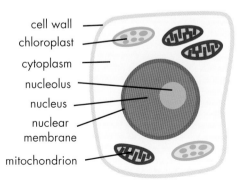

cell wall
chloroplast
cytoplasm
nucleolus
nucleus
nuclear membrane
mitochondrion

Animal Cell

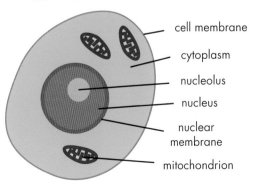

cell membrane
cytoplasm
nucleolus
nucleus
nuclear membrane
mitochondrion

Living barriers

Cell membranes are responsible for keeping cell stuff in and other stuff out—but that doesn't mean the gates are closed permanently. Living cells constantly absorb and release material. They usually use chemical "pumps" to control what enters and exits through the cell membranes. Some things, such as water, can flow freely through the cell membrane—but the cell has to carefully control the flow of water to stay healthy.

One way that water moves through a cell membrane is by a process called osmosis. Imagine that there's a party going on in two rooms that are linked by a door. In the first room, there are a bunch of waiters handing out glasses of water. In the second room, there are thirsty guests, but no waiters with water. The thirsty guests could walk from the second room to the first to get water—unless the door was too itty-bitty to let them through. If the door was just the right size for a glass of water, though, the water glasses could be passed from one room to the other to keep the thirsty guests from keeling over from dehydration. This is roughly how osmosis works. Water passes from the area where there is a lot of it to areas where there isn't enough, until there is an equal amount of water to go around.

You can watch cells "inflate" or "deflate" by placing them in environments of varying water concentrations.

Osmosis: the process by which water passes through a thin layer of material from an area with a higher concentration of water to an area with a lower concentration of water.

Sorry, no room!

EXPERIMENT:
Magic cells that shrink and grow

Watch osmosis in action in real cells.

MATERIALS
- microscope
- microscope slides
- cover slips
- eyedropper
- tweezers
- one onion
- sugar
- water
- measuring spoons and cups
- paper towels

STEP 1: COLLECT THE CELLS.
Use the tweezers to tear off a thin layer of onion skin, as in the first experiment. Lay the skin flat on the microscope slide and place a small drop of water on it. Carefully place a cover slip over the water and onion skin, trying to avoid leaving air bubbles under the cover slip. Soak up any excess liquid carefully with a paper towel.

STEP 2: PREPARE THE SOLUTIONS.
Measure out 1 cup (240 ml) of distilled water (distilled water can be found at the grocery store). Add 6 tablespoons (89 ml) of sugar to the water and mix until the sugar dissolves to make a sugar solution. Measure out a separate cup of distilled water as the fresh water sample.

STEP 3: OBSERVE OSMOSIS.
With your microscope, focus on the onion-skin cells. Use the eyedropper to place a few drops of the sugar solution on one corner of the cover slip. Place a square of paper towel approximately half the size of the slide on the opposite side of the cover slip to help draw the sugar solution under the cover slip. Observe how the onion-skin cells change as the sugar solution washes over them. Do they shrink? (You may have to watch them for several minutes.)

STEP 4: OBSERVE MORE OSMOSIS.

Keep your microscope focused on the onion-skin cells. Use the eyedropper to place a few drops of distilled water onto the same spot where you added the sugar solution. Place a small piece of a paper towel on the opposite side of the cover slip to help draw the fluid under the cover slip. The cells that reacted to the sugar solution in Step 3 will now get a wash of fresh water. Observe how the onion-skin cells change in this step. Do they swell up again?

EXTENSION ACTIVITY: What would happen if you used a contact-lens saline solution in this experiment instead of the sugar solution? Remember, the contact-lens saline solution is a concentration of salt normally found in living tissue.

What's going on?

In this experiment, you can observe osmosis taking place in live cells. When you wash the sugar solution over the onion-skin cells, the cells suddenly have much less water outside than inside. In order to equalize their outside environment to their inside environment, water must flow out of the cells. The end result is a shrinking in size.

In the next step, when fresh water washes over the shrunken onion-skin cells, the cells have less water inside than outside. In this case, the water must rush into the cells, and you can watch them plump up.

Chapter 2
Bacteria in the Kitchen

No matter how much you and your parents clean up, the kitchen will always contain some form of bacteria—you know, those teeny-tiny microorganisms that cover just about everything. Including, of course, this book you're holding!

Where are those little bugs?

Bacteria were discovered circa 1680 by a scientist named Antonie van Leeuwenhoek, who also worked on developing microscopes and discovered sperm cells, blood cells, microscopic organisms called protists, nematodes, and rotifers, and much, much more. He called these organisms "animalcules." His discoveries became the basis of the modern science of microbiology—the study of microorganisms and their effects.

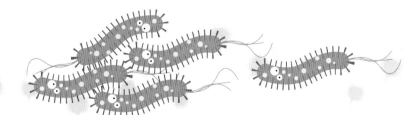

Scientists now know that bacteria come in many shapes, colors, and sizes, although almost all are invisible to the naked eye. Under the microscope, some bacteria, such as *Micrococcus*, look like little balls, while others, such as *Leptospira*, look like tangled strings or corkscrews. There are thousands of types of bacteria in your kitchen. For example, raw chicken is covered in *salmonella* and *campylobacter*—the bacteria most likely to give you food poisoning. Raw ground beef is coated in *Escherichia coli*. Shellfish is just swimming in *Vibrio parahaemolyticus*. That's just a small sampling—there are many more varieties of bacteria in your kitchen at any given moment. That's why it's so important to keep it clean. A dirty kitchen is a playground for bacteria.

MICROCOCCUS

LEPTOSPIRA

SALMONELLA

ESCHERICHIA COLI

CAMPYLOBACTER

VIBRIO PARAHAEMOLYTICUS

Meet a few microscopic organisms

Protists are a group of unicellular organisms that generally live in water and are not plants, animals, or fungi. Instead, they are classified in their own kingdom of organisms, *Protista*, and include things like slime mold, paramecium, amoeba, and golden algae.

Nematodes are worms that are unsegmented and have cylindrical bodies that often narrow at each end. There are about 80,000 species of nematodes.

Rotifers are microscopic multicellular organisms that live in water. They are characterized by a crown of hair-like structures called cilia that they use to propel themselves across water and to move food into their mouths.

SLIME MOLD

PARAMECIUM

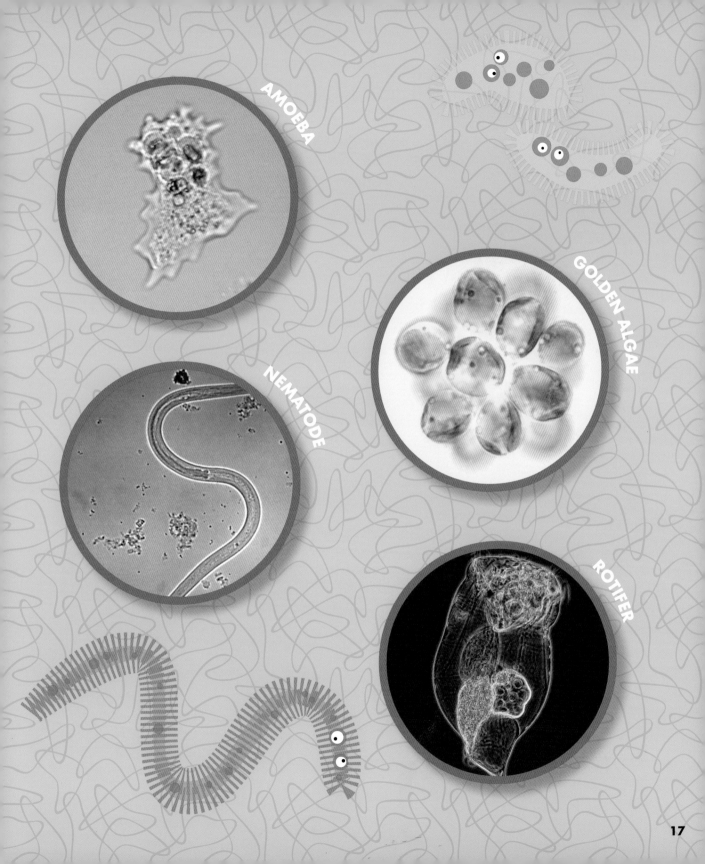

AMOEBA

GOLDEN ALGAE

NEMATODE

ROTIFER

How to make homemade bacterial culture plates

Scientists use Petri dishes—shallow dishes with loose covers—coated with a thin layer of nutrients to culture, or grow, bacteria. You can make your own bacterial culture plates (also called agar plates when they're made with agar, as we'll do here) at home with items from your local market.

MATERIALS
- clear plastic disposable plates (make sure they are not too shallow—if you are concerned that the plates are too shallow, use plastic bowls instead)
- plastic wrap
- one cup (240 ml) of chicken broth
- distilled water
- powdered agar (available in health food stores)
- saucepan
- large wooden spoon for stirring
- oven
- one oven-safe bowl
- one large casserole dish
- oven mitts

STEP 1: PREPARE THE AGAR.
Have an adult help you when using the oven. Set the oven to 300° F (150° C). Pour the chicken broth into the saucepan. Add 2 teaspoons (10 ml) of agar to the saucepan. Mix the agar and broth with the wooden spoon. With an adult's help, slowly heat the mixture on the stovetop until the agar has completely dissolved. Make sure to keep stirring the mixture the whole time it is on the stove. When the agar has dissolved, pour the liquid into the oven-safe bowl. Place the bowl in the casserole dish, and put everything into the oven. (The casserole dish underneath the bowl will catch any spills in case the agar-broth mixture bubbles over.) Heat the mixture in the oven for thirty minutes.

STEP 2: POUR THE PLATES.

Afterward, use the oven mitts to carefully remove the bowl and casserole dish from the oven. Set everything aside to cool for 7–8 minutes. Lay the plastic plates or plastic bowls out on a countertop. Arrange them so you can access them easily—you need to pour the agar mixture quickly before it cools and hardens. Pour a thin layer of the liquid agar into each plate or bowl. Cover them with plastic wrap and set them aside for one hour so that the liquid agar can solidify.

SAFETY FIRST

After you grow bacteria on your culture plates, it is very important that you dispose of the plates completely. Ask an adult to help you, since large amounts of bacteria and other icky things that can grow on these plates can make you sick. To dispose properly, place the plates in a garbage bag. Tie up the bag and place it in a dumpster or leave it out for trash collection. Do not let the plates sit in a household wastebasket after you are done experimenting. Use only disposable materials—don't ever try to wash and reuse the culture plates.

 NOTE: For those of you who can't make your own agar plates from scratch, there are kits available, or you can even buy ready-made culture plates. Both can be found at a science supply store. In fact, you could extend your experiments with agar plates by comparing the plates you make at home to the ones you buy from a supplier. Do they work the same? Is one better for growing germs than the other?

EXPERIMENT: Culturing bacteria

Grow bacteria from different sources.

MATERIALS
- a few agar plates (*See* How to Make Homemade Bacterial Culture Plates, pages 18–19)
- cotton swabs
- distilled water
- masking tape for labels

water

STEP 1: START YOUR CULTURES.

Determine how many bacterial samples you will take, based on how many agar plates you have prepared. You will need one for each sample plus two extras. You can collect bacterial samples from anywhere you'd like. Some places you could swab for bacteria are: the inside of your mouth, the sole of your shoe, the drain of the kitchen sink, a shelf inside the refrigerator, the shower curtain, or your front door. Label each plate with the name of your sample. Label one of the two extra plates "distilled water" and the other plate "no treatment." Pour some distilled water into a clean cup. Dip a few cotton swabs into the distilled water (you need one swab per sample plus one extra swab to test the water itself). With the wet end of the swab, gently wipe the sample sites (such as the shower door or the inside of your mouth) one at a time and then immediately swab the surface of a plate. Be careful when you swab the agar—try not to gouge it or break the surface. Repeat this procedure for each of your samples. For the plate labeled "distilled water," swab its surface with distilled water only. For the plate labeled "no treatment," set it aside and do not swab anything on it. Re-cover the plates with new plastic wrap and set them aside for two days. Make sure they are not disturbed.

STEP 2: EXAMINE THE BACTERIA.

After three days, examine the plates. Record any growths you see, taking note of the texture, color, and shape of the growths. A large "dot" of bacterial growth on a plate is called a colony—

how many colonies grew from your different samples? Did any bacteria grow on the plate labeled "no treatment"? What does this tell you about how sterile (microorganism-free) the conditions were? Did any bacteria grow on the plate labeled "distilled water"? What does this tell you about the quality of distilled water? Which samples grew different types of bacteria? Which samples looked more uniform? Why do you think there were differences?

What's going on?

If the conditions were sterile when you prepared this experiment, the plate labeled "no treatment" should have had no bacterial colonies growing on it. The truth is, though, that it is very difficult to keep things sterile when you are working at home. So don't feel discouraged if your "no treatment" plate had a little guck on it. The same holds for the "distilled water" plate—it shouldn't really have anything on it, if things were sterile, but don't worry about a few dots here and there.

You should have noticed, however, that the plates containing your other samples have a whole horde of stuff growing on them. What the plates look like depends on the type of sample you were testing. For example, bacteria from the sole of your shoe might include lots of types of bacteria because your shoe will carry traces from all the different places you've been, whereas the bacteria from inside your mouth—where temperatures are fairly stable and conditions are largely unchanged—should have colonies that look about the same.

Rotten milk

Let's face it—milk spoils. Everybody knows that. But why does it spoil? Is it magic? Is it some supernatural occurrence? No! It's bacteria!!

EXPERIMENT: Blue milk

How do temperature and time affect the growth of microbes in milk?

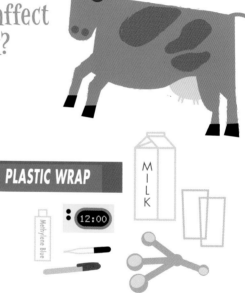

MATERIALS
- clear plastic drinking cups
- teaspoon (for measuring)
- medicine eyedropper
- milk
- plastic wrap
- 1% methylene blue solution (you can buy this at aquarium supply stores—methylene blue can be used to treat fungal infections in aquariums)
- marker
- clock

STEP 1: WORK OUT THE TIMING.
This experiment requires you to leave samples of milk out at room temperature for different amounts of time. It will be easiest if you coordinate the samples to be ready for the methylene blue test all at once. For example, if you want to do your methylene blue test at 7:00 p.m. on Saturday, start setting up your samples on Friday at 7:00 p.m. You should conduct tests at at least five different time periods—milk left out for twenty-four, twelve, six, three, and zero hours—so the samples should be prepared at 7:00 p.m. Friday, 7:00 a.m. Saturday, 1:00 p.m. Saturday, 4:00 p.m. Saturday, and 7:00 p.m. Saturday.

STEP 2: SET UP.
To prepare a sample, add 10 teaspoons (50 ml) of milk to a plastic drinking cup and cover the top with plastic wrap. Mark the time the sample was prepared on the cup, using the marker. Place the cup where it will be out of direct sunlight and will not be disturbed. Prepare the five samples at the times described in Step 1.

STEP 3: THE TEST.

Right after preparing the "zero hours" sample, collect all the cups to perform the methylene blue test. Record the time and then add three drops of 1% methylene blue solution to each cup. Gently swirl the contents of the cups. The milk should turn blue. Examine the samples for the next two days: check them at least once every six hours—but more often if you can—and record the results. Record when each sample changes color from blue back to white. What happened to the color of the samples over time? Which samples changed color most quickly? How does refrigeration affect the freshness of milk?

EXTENSION ACTIVITY: How does contact with spoiled milk affect the rate of microbe growth in fresh milk? Using an eyedropper, add a few drops of spoiled milk to a sample of fresh milk and repeat the methylene blue experiment. Do the colors change on the same time scale as before?

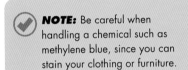 **NOTE:** Be careful when handling a chemical such as methylene blue, since you can stain your clothing or furniture.

What's going on?

Bacteria and other microorganisms (or microbes) are always present in milk. These microbes multiply over time, and they multiply much faster at room temperature than in the refrigerator. Milk microbes need oxygen to survive. In this experiment, methylene blue acted as an indicator to tell you when the oxygen in the milk had been used up. When methylene blue is added to milk, it turns the milk blue, but this color disappears over time as oxygen is used up by the microbes. The higher the concentration of microbes in the milk, the faster the blue color disappears.

EXPERIMENT:
Make an antibacterial cream

Test plant extracts for antibacterial properties.

MATERIALS
- ten agar plates (*See* How to Make a Homemade Bacterial Culture Plates, pages 18–19)
- plastic wrap
- over-the-counter antibacterial ointment
- two thin slices of fresh garlic
- two small leaves of black sage (you can buy this in the spice section of a supermarket)
- two small leaves of grass
- saliva
- twelve cotton swabs
- a few clean drinking glasses
- rubbing alcohol
- tweezers

STEP 1: PREPARE THE PLATES.
Rinse a drinking glass with rubbing alcohol. After the alcohol has completely evaporated, spit into the glass and collect a few teaspoons of saliva. Dip ten cotton swabs into the saliva. With the wet end of one swab, gently wipe saliva all over the surface of an agar plate. Repeat this procedure using a new saliva swab for each of the nine other agar plates. Cover the plates with plastic wrap, and set them aside for two days. Make sure they are not disturbed. After two days, there should be a uniform growth of bacteria over the surface of each of the plates.

 NOTE: You can do this experiment using other herbs (such as ginger, cumin, turmeric, pepper, lavender, oregano, or anything else you have on hand) from your kitchen if garlic, sage, or grass are not available.

STEP 2: TEST THE ANTIBACTERIALS.

Set aside the slice of garlic, the small leaf of black sage, and the small blade of grass. Arrange all the agar plates from Step 1 so you have easy access to them. Remove the plastic wrap and dispose of it. Pour a small amount of rubbing alcohol into a clean drinking glass. Dip the tips of the tweezers into the rubbing alcohol and let them dry. Use the tweezers to place one slice of garlic in the center of one of the plates. Dip the tweezers in the alcohol again and let them dry. Repeat this procedure for the black sage and the grass (or any other herbs that you've chosen to experiment with), allotting one item per agar plate. Squeeze a small drop of over-the-counter antibacterial ointment in the center of two agar plates. Leave the remaining two agar plates untouched. Cover the plates with new plastic wrap and set them aside for one day.

STEP 3: : CHECK FOR ANTIBACTERIAL STRENGTH.

After the potential antibacterial samples have interacted with the bacteria for a day, examine the plates. Look for clear areas around the edges of the potential antibacterial samples—if the area is clear, it indicates that the bacterial colonies are dead. Are there large clear areas around the edges of the dollops of over-the-counter antibacterial ointment? Are these the largest clear areas of all the samples? Are the clear areas around the garlic larger than those around the black sage? Were there any clear areas around the grass? Does this suggest that one of the samples has more antibacterial power than the others?

What's going on?

You already know that antibacterial ointment kills bacteria—after all, that's why the manufacturer calls it "antibacterial" on the package. The over-the-counter antibacterial ointment was this experiment's positive control—it showed you what an antibacterial substance should do to the bacteria on the agar plates. The untreated plates were the negative control—they showed you what happens when there is absolutely no antibacterial activity present.

Of the three plants you tested in this experiment, garlic is the most powerful antibacterial agent, whereas grass is the least powerful. Garlic has chemicals in it that are able to kill bacteria—in fact, the same chemicals that kill bacteria are the ones that give garlic its smell. (Of course, the smell is enough to keep us from making garlic soap!) The clear area on the plate surrounding each plant should correspond to its antibacterial strength.

Positive Control: a procedure that is very similar to the actual experimental test but is known from previous experiments to give a positive result. A positive control confirms that the experimental conditions are able to produce a positive result.

Negative Control: in an experiment, this reveals what happens when essentially nothing is tested. A negative control is known to give a negative result. In most cases, the value of the negative control can be thought of as a background value to be subtracted from the test sample results.

Chapter 3
Fungus Among Us

Bacteria are not the only creepy critters around us all the time—fungus is in no short supply. Fungus is everywhere. It often grows larger than microscopic bacteria—fungus can grow into fuzzy, colorful, or solid forms. Think about the green mold you might find on old bread in the back of the fridge—or think of a mushroom! Both are examples of fungi. There is a wide range of fungus to be found: diseases like athlete's foot fungus, corn smut, and wheat rust can be caused by fungi, while other fungi are used to make antibiotics and cheese.

One type of fungus that you can find all over the place, especially in your kitchen, is yeast. Yeast are interesting critters—they are single-celled organisms that can do everything from causing disease to making bread rise. Yeast has been used by humans for so long that archaeologists digging in ancient Egyptian ruins have discovered grinding stones and baking chambers for breads baked with yeast. They have also found drawings of four-thousand-year-old bakeries.

There are a thousand types of yeast (but don't worry—only a few of them are harmful to your health). The size of yeast cells varies, but the average cells are between 4 and 12 micrometers long. Exactly how big is that? Well, the finest human hairs are about 25 micrometers wide, so yeast cells are only a fraction of that.

EXPERIMENT: Bud your yeast

Examine how yeast cells reproduce.

MATERIALS
- one package of active dry yeast
- one cup (240 ml) of warm water
- one bowl
- one spoon
- 1 tablespoon (15 ml) of sugar
- microscope
- microscope slides and cover slips
- 1% methylene blue solution (available at aquarium supply stores)
- eyedropper

STEP 1: MAKE THE BUDS.
Mix the water, active dry yeast, and sugar in the bowl. Set the mixture aside for 45 minutes.

STEP 2: WATCH THEM GROW.
After the mixture has been sitting for 45 minutes, add 10 drops of methylene blue to the bowl and stir gently with the spoon. Then place a medium-size drop of this mixture on a microscope slide. Cover the liquid carefully with a cover slip, making sure no air bubbles are trapped. Examine the yeast cells under different magnifications on the microscope. Make note of differences in cell sizes. Are most of the yeast cells uniform in size? Do you occasionally spot a smaller yeast cell attached to a larger cell?

EXTENSION ACTIVITY: What happens if you don't add sugar to the bowl of water and active yeast? Do you see any evidence of budding without the presence of sugar? What does this prove about yeast cells' need for nutrients in order to grow?

What's going on?

Yeast cells reproduce very quickly, and, most of the time, they reproduce in one of two ways: fission, or budding. Fission is a process by which a single yeast cell splits into two individual cells, which then grow and reproduce on their own. Budding is a process in which a part of the yeast's cell wall swells and forms a new growth called a bud. The bud then breaks off and becomes an independent cell. The original yeast cell is called the mother cell; the newly formed cell that buds off from the mother is called the daughter cell. This is a form of asexual reproduction, since only one parent is required to create offspring.

When you view growing yeast cells through a microscope, you should be able to see budding in process—can you see smaller cells attached to the larger ones? That's budding! Fission isn't as easy to view at home, but that's happening, too.

Respiration

Fungi such as yeast may seem like simple organisms, but in truth they must do very complex things in order to live and survive. Turning food into energy is probably the most important of these tasks. Sugars and carbohydrates are common foods for yeast.

Yeast cells use their food and the oxygen from the air to produce carbon dioxide, water, and energy. This process is called aerobic respiration, which is the same process that the cells in the human body use for energy. Even when there is no oxygen around, though, yeast cells are able to make energy. In the absence of oxygen, they use a different process called anaerobic respiration. In anaerobic respiration, sugar is broken down and used to make carbon dioxide, alcohol, and energy. It is a pretty nifty trick to be able to make energy without oxygen, but it comes at a price—compared to aerobic respiration, anaerobic respiration produces far less energy. To make things worse for the yeast, the alcohol produced during anaerobic respiration is toxic to the cells. Over time, if the yeast cells use only anaerobic respiration for energy, they will all die.

EXPERIMENT: Balloon blow-up

Use yeast to inflate a balloon.

MATERIALS
- six packages of active dry yeast
- 2 cups (480 ml) of very cold water
- 2 cups (473 ml) of very hot, but not boiling, water
- 2 cups (480 ml) of warm water
- 6 tablespoons (90 ml) of sugar
- six small plastic soda bottles
- six latex balloons
- tape
- marker
- tape measure

STEP 1: ASSEMBLE THE BOTTLES.
Empty and rinse the soda bottles. Add one packet of yeast to each bottle. Add 1 cup (240 ml) of cold water to each of two bottles. Add 1 cup (240 ml) of hot water to each of the next two bottles. Add 1 cup (240 ml) of warm water to each of the final two bottles. Label the bottles "cold," "hot," or "warm." Add 1 tablespoon of sugar to one of each of the "cold," "hot," and "warm" bottles and label those bottles "with sugar." DO NOT add sugar to the other bottles. Swirl each soda bottle around to mix the ingredients. Attach a balloon over the mouth of each bottle. You can add some tape around the mouths of the bottles to secure the balloons in place.

STEP 2: WATCH THE BALLOONS.
Observe the bottles. What happens to the balloons after five minutes? After fifteen minutes? After thirty minutes? Use the tape measure to determine the girth of the balloons (measure them at their widest point) as they inflate (or not). Over time, does the balloon on the warm-water bottle with sugar inflate? Do the balloons on the bottles without sugar inflate? How do those balloons compare to the other ones with sugar?

What's going on?

In this experiment, covering the bottle with a balloon cuts off the oxygen supply to the yeast. For a while, the yeast cells use aerobic respiration for energy. When the trapped oxygen runs out, though, they switch to anaerobic respiration.

Carbon dioxide is also made during this process (although it doesn't give the organism any energy), and that is what inflates the balloons. Since carbon dioxide is also a by-product of aerobic respiration, the balloons will begin to inflate even before the oxygen runs out. As carbon dioxide continues to be produced, the balloons continue to inflate, which proves that yeast cells can respirate anaerobically.

Neither form of respiration will take place without a food source—in this case, the sugar. That's why the balloons over the bottles with yeast but no sugar do not inflate—their yeast cells are not respiring.

By testing different water temperatures, you can examine how other external factors affect the way cells function. You probably noticed that the balloons over the bottles of hot and cold water did not inflate as much as the one over the bottle of warm water. What does this tell you about the temperature that's best for cells to grow?

Mold: Not as innocent as you may think

Yeast is not the only fungus out there. You're probably familiar with another fungus—mold. The bluish-greenish stuff on that old loaf of bread or that blackish-brown gunk on old fruit are both different types of mold.

Molds are often considered a nuisance, forcing us to throw food away and clean our kitchens. But mold can be more than an inconvenience—it can be dangerous. Mold can destroy crops, which can lead to food shortages. Mold can cause allergic reactions, which can lead to breathing problems. And under the right conditions, some molds produce poisonous substances (called mycotoxins) that can really make you sick. Sometimes the toxins produced by a mold can survive for a long time and withstand high temperatures, so be very careful around mold.

How molds eat

Molds digest the things they "eat" by producing special proteins called enzymes and secreting these enzymes outside their cells onto the food source. The enzymes break down large food-source molecules into smaller molecules that can be transported into the cells of the mold. Inside the cells, the molecules are further broken down to provide the mold with energy. When molds rot things such as wood or food, they literally digest their way through the material.

EXPERIMENT:

How does your mold garden grow?

Explore the perfect conditions for growing mold.

MATERIALS
- one apple, cut into ten pieces
- one slice of bread, cut into ten pieces
- ten small, clean jars (such as baby food jars)
- 4 tablespoons (60 ml) of salt
- 2 tablespoons (30 ml) of water
- 2 tablespoons (30 ml) of vinegar
- 1 tablespoon (15 ml) of dish detergent
- marker

STEP 1: SEED THE MOLD GARDEN.
Label the jars as follows: "sunlight, untreated"; "dark, untreated"; "sunlight, water"; "dark, water"; "sunlight, salt"; "dark, salt"; "sunlight, vinegar"; "dark, vinegar"; "sunlight, dish detergent"; and "dark, dish detergent." Add one piece of apple and one piece of bread to each jar. Add 1 tablespoon (15 ml) of water to the jars marked "water." Add 1 tablespoon (15 ml) of vinegar to the jars marked "vinegar." Add 2 tablespoons (30 ml) of salt to the jars marked "salt." Add 1 tablespoon (15 ml) of dish detergent to the jars marked "dish detergent." Leave the remaining two jars untreated. Replace the lids on all the jars. Place the jars marked "sunlight" on a sunny windowsill. Place the jars marked "dark" in a dark closet or basement.

It is very important that after you grow your mold garden, you dispose of it completely, since large amounts of mold and other icky things can make you sick. To dispose properly, place the jars in a garbage bag. Tie up the bag and place it in a dumpster or leave it out for trash collection. Do not let the jars sit in a household wastebasket after you are done experimenting. Don't wash and reuse the jars—use only disposable materials in this experiment.

STEP 2: WATCH IT GROW.

Examine the jars once a day for two weeks and record the results. What changes do you observe? Do the different types of food have different types of mold growing on them? Does more mold grow in sunlight or in the dark? Do any of the additives have an effect on the rate of mold growth or the types of mold you see?

What's going on?

Within a few weeks, you should start to notice a smattering of things growing in your mold garden. But the things you added and where the jars were left made a difference in how much mold grew. Molds grow best in warm, dark, moist conditions—did you observe this in your experiment? Also, salt and vinegar are natural preservatives—they prevent food from spoiling—so they should have decreased the amount of mold that grew.

Did this experiment teach you something about why it is such a bad idea to lose your lunch bag at the back of your locker? Perhaps you should plan to bring that home on a more regular basis. . . .

The secret of the mummy

Now that you know something about bacteria and fungi, you can explore ways to keep them from growing. Throughout history, humans have often lost the battle against spreading bacteria and fungi—for example, the bubonic plague, which was believed to have been caused by a bacterium called *Yersinia pestis*, killed twenty-five million people in Europe in the fourteenth century. Another example concerns a fungus that grows on the plant rye called *Claviceps purpurea*. Once this fungus infects the rye, a highly toxic disease called ergot develops. Attacks of this disease have occurred throughout recorded history, or at least since 854 A.D. People who ate the infected rye (after it was made into things like bread) suffered intense burning pains in their limbs, which then quickly became diseased and fell off. The disease, now known as ergotism, was called Holy Fire— "holy" because people believed it was a punishment from God and "fire" for the burning sensations. Thousands of people have died of the disease, and the survivors are left horribly mutilated.

Nevertheless, several ancient cultures were very successful in fighting bacteria and fungi. Notably, the ancient Egyptians were able to preserve their dead relatives as mummies. Make your own mummy in your kitchen and see if you can figure out THE SECRET OF THE MUMMY.

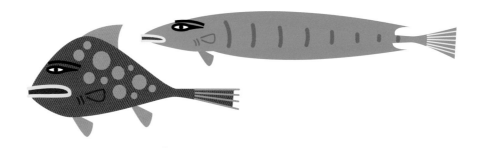

EXPERIMENT: The mummy

Make a mummy from a fish (a dead fish, that is).

MATERIALS
- one small fish that has been scaled and gutted (you can get one at a fish store or supermarket)
- one plastic container large enough to totally submerge the fish
- two 2-pound boxes of baking soda
- measuring tape
- kitchen scale

STEP 1: PREPARE THE FISH.
Weigh the fish on the kitchen scale. Measure it from head to tail. Record these measurements. Also, record the fish's general appearance. Is the skin shiny or dull? What is its general color and smell?

STEP 2: PREPARE THE SARCOPHAGUS.
Pour a 2-inch (5-cm) layer of baking soda into the plastic container. Pack the fish's gut cavity with baking soda—pack the baking soda all around the interior, but be careful not to damage the fish. Place the fish inside the plastic container, on top of the layer of baking soda. Pour more baking soda into the container to totally submerge the fish in baking soda. There should be a 2-inch (5-cm) layer of baking soda all around the fish.

STEP 3: BURY THE MUMMY.
Place the plastic container in a place where it won't be disturbed for a week. After one week, take the fish

SAFETY FIRST

ALWAYS remember to wash your hands thoroughly with soap after handling raw fish.

out and examine its appearance. Record your observations. Clean the baking soda out of the gut cavity and weigh the fish. Record the weight. Measure its length and record that as well. Pack the fish in fresh baking soda and put it back in the container for another week. Record your observations about the fish's appearance, weight, and length after a total of two weeks in baking soda.

What's going on?

The mummified fish will change drastically after two weeks in baking soda. After one week, the fish will weigh less and feel rougher. After two weeks, the fish will have lost about half its body weight and will feel leathery. The baking soda is not quite what ancient Egyptians used on their relatives— they used a naturally occurring chemical called natron, which is found on the banks of the Nile. Baking soda and natron act similarly, however—both absorb water.

If you were to examine the baking soda that was closest to the fish in the plastic container, you would feel a bit of moisture. The baking soda dehydrated the fish's body as it absorbed the water from the fish's tissues and cells. This helped to preserve, or mummify, the body.

All living things, including bacteria and fungi, require water to live. A dead fish left exposed to air without being dehydrated will soon decay— that's part of the stink in a fish store. Microorganisms grow on the dead tissue, creating a strong, unpleasant odor. By dehydrating the fish, the growth of bacteria and fungi is slowed down—with less water available, fewer microorganisms can grow.

Now you know the secret of mummification!

Chapter 4
Kitchen Chemistry

There is a lot of biology on display in your kitchen—you know that fact well by now. You may not realize, however, that your kitchen is also a fully stocked chemistry lab. Cooking is a fine example of chemistry in your kitchen. Mixing ingredients together often involves chemistry—and chemistry sometimes happens when things are left alone. Explore for yourself!

Acids and bases

Performing kitchen-chemistry experiments will require a knowledge of acids and bases. What are these? Well, scientists define acids and bases in relation to the balance of protons (positively charged particles) and electrons (negatively charged particles) in a solution. Solutions that have an excess of protons are acidic. Solutions that have too few protons are basic. Some acids, like battery acid, are very potent. Bases like drain cleaner are also very powerful. Strong acids and bases can be dangerous and must be handled with care. For the most part, the acids and bases that you have in your kitchen don't pose a danger—but knowing which is which can help when you're cooking or cleaning. For example, if you wanted to make a cream of tomato soup, you'd have to add milk to cooked tomatoes. Tomatoes are slightly acidic, and if you add acid to milk, it curdles—hardly appetizing. But if you add a pinch of baking soda to the tomatoes first to neutralize their acidity (baking soda is basic) and then add the milk, you get a creamy delicious soup.

Here's a quick and easy way to tell an acid from a base—acids taste sour and bases taste bitter. Of course, please don't go tasting everything in your kitchen to tell your acids from your bases—there are better ways to figure that out. The pH scale was devised to describe how acidic or basic something is. Acids have a pH below 7. Neutral solutions, in which there are equal amounts of protons and electrons, have a pH of exactly 7. Basic solutions have a pH above 7.

EXPERIMENT: Cabbage juice indicator

Make a colorific pH indicator.

MATERIALS
- one head of red cabbage
- grater
- large bowl
- pot for boiling
- strainer
- water
- five paper cups
- lemon juice
- milk
- liquid dish detergent
- baking soda

STEP 1: COOK THE CABBAGE.
Grate about one half of the head of red cabbage into the pot. Add water until the grated cabbage is covered. Boil the cabbage in the water for about half an hour. Afterward, let the hot cabbage-water sit for another half hour, until the liquid cools down enough to handle. Strain the mixture over the large bowl and collect the dark bluish-purple liquid. Dispose of the cabbage (or eat it with dinner!).

STEP 2: TEST THE INDICATOR.
Pour about 3 tablespoons (45 ml) of cabbage juice into each of the five paper cups. You will use the cups to test the pH of the four sample liquids. Label the cups "control," "lemon juice," "milk," "detergent," and "soda." Add nothing to the cabbage juice in the cup labeled "control," since this cup will be the standard by which to compare the other sample liquids in the experiment. Add 1 tablespoon (15 ml) of each of the liquid samples to the appropriately labeled cups. Record any color changes you see.

What's going on?

Chemicals that change in some noticeable way—for example, change in color—when exposed to substances of different pH levels are called pH indicators. Red cabbage contains pigments called anthocyanins that are sensitive to pH. The anthocyanins in red cabbage take on the following colors at different pH values:

pH		APPROXIMATE COLOR
2		Red
4		Purple
6		Violet
8		Blue
10		Green
12		Greenish-yellow

During this experiment, you will have noticed that when you mixed the cabbage juice with an acidic solution like lemon juice, it turned bright pink. When you mixed it with a basic solution like dish detergent, it turned green. What did you discover about the pH of milk and soda?

EXPERIMENT: Turmeric indicator

Other things in the kitchen can act as pH indicators.

MATERIALS
- 1 teaspoon (5 ml) of turmeric, which you can buy in your supermarket's spice section
- 1 cup (240 ml) of rubbing alcohol
- two bowls
- 1 teaspoon (5 ml) of baking soda
- ½ cup (120 ml) of water
- ½ cup (120 ml) of white vinegar

STEP 1: MAKE THE INDICATOR.
In one of the bowls, mix the turmeric and the rubbing alcohol.

STEP 2: TEST IT!
In the other bowl, mix the water and baking soda. Pour some of the turmeric-alcohol mixture into the second bowl. Add just enough to cause the liquids to change colors. Did the mixture turn red? Then, slowly pour the vinegar into the baking soda mixture. Record what happens to the liquids. Add a little more vinegar. Did the mixture begin to foam and then turn yellow?

Be careful when handling a chemical such as alcohol, as it can be extremely flammable.

What's going on?

Just like the cabbage juice, the turmeric-alcohol mixture is a pH indicator. It does, however, have different properties. The color changes that happen in response to acids or bases are different from the color scale of the red cabbage reactions. In solutions that are acidic, the turmeric–alcohol mixture stays yellow, but in basic solutions the mixture turns red.

One neat thing about the turmeric-alcohol indicator is that the color-change reaction is reversible. You saw this for yourself in the experiment. Baking soda is basic, so when you mixed the turmeric-alcohol indicator with the baking soda solution, the whole thing turned red. When you added vinegar to the mix, the acidic vinegar first reacted with the baking soda to neutralize it. The bubbles you saw were the result of the neutralization reaction that produced carbon dioxide gas. Then, when you added more vinegar than was needed to neutralize the baking soda, the solution became acidic. This caused the turmeric-alcohol indicator to change back to yellow.

Powerful chemicals

Acids and bases can be extremely powerful. Upon hearing the word "acid," many people immediately think of a container with noxious smoke and poisonous vapors rising out of it. They imagine a liquid that would burn like fire if it touched their skin or that would dissolve any material on contact. The truth is not quite as exciting,  although many acids are indeed just that strong. For example, sulfuric acid (the liquid in car batteries) can easily eat a hole in a piece of iron, as well as eat through your clothes and skin. And your stomach is full of strong acids that help break down and digest the food you have eaten. Concentrated stomach acid can irritate your stomach lining and even eat a hole in it. For some reason, bases don't get the same amount of respect, even though they are just as capable of burning like fire or eating through skin and clothes. Some free advice: stay away from strong bases such as concentrated sodium hydroxide (lye, found in some plumbing products).

Even the relatively weak acids and bases that you find in your kitchen can cause some substantial changes. Try vinegar, for example, and just add an egg. . . .

EXPERIMENT: Naked eggs

Remove an eggshell with chemistry.

MATERIALS
- one raw egg
- 2-cup (480 ml) measuring bowl/cup
- 1½ cups (360 ml) of vinegar

STEP 1: PREPARE THE BATH.
Carefully place the egg inside the measuring bowl. Pour vinegar into the measuring bowl until it covers the egg. Do you notice any tiny bubbles floating off the eggshell as soon as it is immersed in the vinegar? Wait two days.

STEP 2: OOH! IT'S NAKED!
After two days, carefully remove the egg from the vinegar bath. Place it gently on a countertop. Is the eggshell still there? Is the egg now translucent and soft?

What's going on?

When you dip the egg in the vinegar bath, a whole lot of chemistry starts happening between the acidic vinegar and the chemicals in the eggshell. One chemical compound in particular is affected by the vinegar: calcium carbonate, which makes eggshells hard.

Vinegar is an acid. When the eggshell came into contact with the vinegar, a chemical reaction took place between the calcium carbonate in the eggshell and the acetic acid. This reaction produced carbon dioxide gas, which caused the bubbles you saw, and took some of the calcium carbonate out of the eggshell. This left the eggshell soft and rubbery. If you left the egg in the vinegar long enough, the shell completely dissolved, leaving behind only the thin membrane that separates the egg from the rest of the world.

Don't forget the bases!

Vinegar is an acid, but it isn't just acids that can cause super changes. Bleach is a common household base—your parents may use it for laundry or for disinfecting the house. Try another experiment with bleach and some bones . . . chicken bones, that is.

EXPERIMENT: How brittle are bones?

Explore what happens to a chicken bone in bleach sauce.

MATERIALS
- four chicken wing bones, cleaned of any meat
- two small jars with lids
- bleach
- water
- a marker
- scissors
- tweezers
- goggles
- rubber gloves

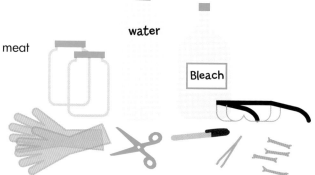

STEP 1: PREPARE THE BATH.
Use the marker to label one jar "water" and the other "bleach." Put on your goggles and your rubber gloves. Fill the jars as labeled, with either the water or the bleach (have your grown-up assistant handle the bleach). Drop two of the chicken bones in the water jar and the other two bones in the bleach jar. Close the lids on the jars. Leave the bones in the jars for one day.

STEP 2: ARE THE BONES BROKEN AFTER A DAY?
After one day, remove one of the bones submerged in bleach with the tweezers (again, have your grown-up assistant handle the bleach). Rinse the bone under running water for two minutes. Examine this bone, as well as one of the bones that had been submerged in water. Test their flexibility and strength and examine their appearance. Use the scissors to try to cut the bones. Record whether they are easy or difficult to cut.

You must have an adult's help for this experiment to supervise the use of bleach. Be careful when handling chemicals such as bleach, since direct contact with skin can be harmful.

STEP 3: ARE THE BONES BROKEN AFTER TWO DAYS?

Continue to soak the remaining bones in each jar, and then remove them with the tweezers. Again, remember to rinse any bones that were submerged in bleach under running water for two minutes. Examine the appearance of the bones and test their flexibility and strength. Also try to cut the bones again. Is the bone that was submerged in bleach dry and brittle after one day? Is it more so after two days? Has the bone submerged in water changed at all after two days? Are the bleach-dipped bones easy to cut with the scissors? Is the water-dipped bone difficult to cut?

What's going on?

You might already know that calcium is important for keeping bones hard and strong. (Remember the Naked Egg experiment? It was the calcium carbonate in the eggshells that kept them hard.) But as important as calcium is, it alone is not enough to keep your bones working the way they should. Bones are full of protein fibers that are just as important to their function as calcium.

When you submerged the chicken bones in bleach, you started a chemical reaction that broke down most of the proteins and tissues. All that was left was the calcium and other minerals—which by themselves aren't enough to make strong bones!

Protective chemistry

The possibilities for kitchen chemistry experiments are endless and extend beyond acids, bases, and neutralization reactions. A very common chemical reaction that happens in kitchens around the globe is the browning of perfectly good apples.

Every cell in an apple contains a chemical called polyphenol oxidase (PPO). When an apple is sliced, some of its cells are opened. This causes the PPO to be exposed to the air, which forces PPO to undergo a chemical reaction with the oxygen in the air. This process is known as oxidation. Oxidation is what makes the brown color appear on apple slices.

Kitchen chemistry is responsible for apple browning, but can it also protect apples? Let's find out more!

Oxidation: the chemical reaction that takes place when a substance combines with oxygen atoms.

EXPERIMENT:
Hey, Apple! Orange you glad to see me?

Use an orange to prevent an apple from browning.

MATERIALS
- one apple
- one orange
- orange juice
- knife
- three bowls

STEP 1: PREPARE THE FRUIT.
With an adult's help, cut three flat slices of apple. Also cut a small slice of orange, making sure it is smaller than the surface of the apple slices.

STEP 2: ASSEMBLE THE FRUIT.
Place the apple slices in the bowls, one slice in each bowl. Pour a little orange juice over the first slice. Place the orange slice over the center of the second apple slice. Leave the last slice alone.

STEP 3: CHECK FOR BROWNING.
Leave the bowls out for two hours. Afterward, remove the apple slices from the bowls and record any changes in their appearances. Did the uncovered apple slice turn brown? Did the apple slice coated in orange juice stay free of browning? Did the portion of the apple slice under the orange slice stay free of browning?

What's going on?

Since you know that oxidation is responsible for apple browning, you probably figured out that stopping oxidation would also stop the browning of apples. One way to prevent oxidation is to stop oxygen from reaching the PPO molecules in the cells. In this experiment, you blocked the oxygen by adding ascorbic acid (also known as vitamin C) to the apples to prevent the chemical reaction from taking place.

Orange juice contains a lot of ascorbic acid. Placing an apple slice in contact with the orange slice or coating an apple slice in orange juice introduces ascorbic acid into the apple cells. Also, the orange slice and juice act as barriers to air, preventing oxygen from reaching the PPO molecules.

Play with your food

There is science all over the kitchen. Mind-boggling, isn't it? All you need to do to get a healthy dose of science is open your refrigerator and this book!

The food in your kitchen can be used to do a variety of fun and amazing experiments. Just pull up a chair and settle down at the counter while a full helping of science is served right up!

Scream for ice cream

Did you know that the average American eats about 15 quarts (14.2 liters) of ice cream every year? It's easy to make homemade ice cream and it turns out that the process of making ice cream is a very important educational tool. Really.

EXPERIMENT: Homemade ice cream

Make ice cream to learn about the phases of matter.

MATERIALS
- 1 tablespoon (15 ml) of sugar
- ½ cup (120 ml) of whole milk
- ¼ teaspoon (1 ml) of vanilla extract
- one saucepan
- one clean stirring spoon
- 6 tablespoons (90 ml) of rock salt (available in most hardware stores or supermarkets)
- one pint-size (½-liter) zipper-sealed plastic bag
- one gallon-size (4-liter) zipper-sealed plastic bag
- crushed ice

 You must have an adult's help for this experiment to supervise the cooking.

STEP 1: COMBINING AND COOKING.
Cleanliness is very important in the process of making ice cream, so make sure the saucepan and spoon are clean and that you use only new zipper bags. Combine the sugar, whole milk, and vanilla extract in the saucepan. With an adult's help, cook the mixture on low heat until everything is well combined and the milk just starts to boil. Stir with the mixing spoon as needed during this phase.

STEP 2: COOLING AND MIXING.
Fill the large (gallon-size) zipper bag about halfway full of ice. Add the rock salt to the ice in the bag. Add the sugar, milk, and vanilla mixture from the previous step to the small (pint-size) zippered bag and seal it. Place the small bag inside the larger bag. Carefully shake the large bag back and forth for ten minutes in order to thoroughly mix everything up.

STEP 3: HARDENING.
Afterward, let everything stand undisturbed for another five minutes to allow the ice cream to harden. Then the small bag can be removed, wiped dry, and opened. What does the mixture inside look like? What does it taste like?

What's going on?

Making ice cream in this way is an excellent demonstration of kitchen chemistry. There are four important components to ice cream that come together to give it the correct texture and consistency. First, there is a liquid component that consists of dissolved sugars, salts, and milk proteins (which give the ice cream its flavor). This liquid component is important in keeping the ice cream from freezing into a solid block of ice. The second component is made up of solid ice crystals, which trap the other ingredients between them to stabilize the ice cream. The third component is milk fat, which gives the ice cream smoothness. The last component is actually a gas—trapped air bubbles that make the mixture lighter and smoother. When you're making good ice cream, you need to combine these four components in the proper proportions.

The components get mixed in three separate steps. The first step is just combining the ingredients and cooking them over heat. The second step involves cooling the cooked ingredients to a temperature below the freezing point of water, and more thorough mixing. Step three gives the ice cream its correct consistency through hardening.

Full of hot air

Ice cream isn't the only food that combines different phases of matter—marshmallows, a fireside favorite, do as well. You can think of the solid parts of the marshmallow as a flexible container full of air. And when air gets hot, things get popping. . . .

EXPERIMENT:
The great growing marshmallow

What happens when you heat a marshmallow?

MATERIALS
- four normal or jumbo-size marshmallows
- paper towels
- a microwave

STEP 1: HOT.
Place the first marshmallow on a paper towel in the microwave. Heat it on the highest setting for ten seconds. How does it look after heating compared to the unheated marshmallows? Did it expand in size? Let the marshmallow cool to room temperature. Record how it changes in appearance and texture.

STEP 2: HOTTER.
Place the second marshmallow on a paper towel in the microwave. Heat it on the highest setting for thirty seconds. How does it look after heating compared to the unheated marshmallows? Did it also expand in size—more than the first marshmallow? Let the marshmallow cool to room temperature and note any changes in appearance and texture.

 Have an adult supervise this experiment, since the marshmallow may get very hot.

STEP 3: HOTTEST.

Place the third marshmallow on a paper towel in the microwave. Heat it for fifty seconds. Compare its appearance after heating to the unheated marshmallows and also to the first and second marshmallows. In addition, let it cool and record any changes. Which of the three marshmallows expanded the most? Did heating the marshmallows for longer cause them to expand more, or did they melt? What happens as the heated marshmallows cool? Do they return to their normal size and shape?

What's going on?

When air inside a closed container is heated, its molecules begin to move more quickly and exert more pressure on the sides of the container. In effect, the hot air tries to expand, and when it is enclosed in a flexible container—such as a marshmallow—it can push against the container enough to make the container expand as well. This experiment is a good demonstration of Charles's Law, which states that the volume—the amount of space something takes up—of a gas increases when its temperature increases.

Charles's Law: based on the work of scientist Jacques Charles, this law states that at constant pressure, the volume of a gas increases when the temperature rises. When the temperature drops, the volume of the gas decreases.

Architecture in the kitchen

No, we're not talking about whether your parents have wood cabinets or granite counters—but the same architectural principles used to keep buildings from falling down are also naturally occurring in your kitchen. A classic example is the eggshell. Have you ever wondered how birds can sit on their eggs and not break them? The answer lies in the shape of the egg.

EXPERIMENT: Super-strong shells

How much weight can be balanced on eggshells?

MATERIALS
- four raw eggs
- Scotch tape
- scissors with thin, fine points (such as cuticle scissors)
- one dinner plate
- about two dozen large, heavy nails

STEP 1: BUILD THE BASE.
Carefully make a small hole at the bottom of each egg, rather than cracking them at the middle. You can ask an adult to use the tip of a pair of nail scissors to puncture the shells. Empty the shells of their contents. (By all means, cook and eat the contents!) Rinse the shells with water and pat them dry. Apply Scotch tape around the middle of each eggshell. Cut the eggshells along the taped ring around the eggshell to make four eggshell domes. Arrange the eggshell domes into a square on a flat surface with the cut sides down.

STEP 2: BALANCE WEIGHT.
Balance the dinner plate over the eggshell domes. Begin adding the nails to the dinner plate, one at a time. See how many nails you can add to the plate before the eggs break. Is it more weight than you expected?

Architecturally speaking, eggs are eggscellent. The arch shape distributes any weight laid on top evenly across the entire arch structure. Arch-shaped eggshells can support a lot of weight because the load is supported by the whole shell instead of just one point on the shell. Do you want more proof of the strength of an arch? Check out the Roman aqueducts. These structures were huge—for example, the aqueduct in Segovia, Spain, is part of a water supply system that is 10 miles (16 kilometers) long. It spans a half-mile (800 meter) valley and is 90 feet (28 meters) tall at its highest point. It is built entirely from granite—there is no mortar or other adhesive connection between individual stones. The arch is so strong that the aqueduct is still able to support thousands of gallons of water, after nearly a two-thousand-year career.

The ancient Roman aqueduct in Segovia, Spain.

Electrical sources

Electricity can do big things—but it is created by one of the smallest things in the world, the electron. Electrons are tiny particles that help make up atoms (the other parts of atoms are protons and neutrons). The number of electrons, protons, and neutrons inside an atom determines what kind of atom it is. Each electron has a slight electric charge, and when a group of them—a very, very large group—surges through a metal wire, an electrical current is formed. To give you an idea of how many electrons are used to power the items around your house, consider this: it takes approximately six million million million electrons, or six quintillion electrons, to light a lightbulb for just one second. By the way, that number again is:

6,000,000,000,000,000,000!

What a shock!

By now, it's no shock that your kitchen is brimming with potential science experiments. But would it surprise you to know that you can use your kitchen to make electricity? No, not by plugging something into a wall outlet—simply by using foods such as lemons and potatoes. Not every food can serve as a battery. Bread won't work. Neither will carrots. Only certain foods will work—and a lemon works particularly well. See why in the next experiment.

EXPERIMENT: Bitter battery

Power up with a lemon.

MATERIALS

- one lemon
- one galvanized nail (ask at the hardware store for this since it is a particular type of nail with a zinc coating)
- one penny
- copper wire (you can get this from any hardware store)
- alligator clips
- flashlight bulb
- small knife

SAFETY FIRST You must have an adult's help for this experiment to supervise the cutting.

STEP 1: BUILD THE BATTERY

Roll the lemon around on a table, pushing down on it gently—but make sure you do not break the peel. This will mash up the inside of the lemon. Stick a penny and a nail into the lemon. Place them close together, but make sure that they do not touch. You will need an adult to cut small slits for the penny in the lemon peel with a knife. Just for giggles, stick out your tongue and touch the penny and nail with it at the same time (make sure the penny and the nail are clean!). Do you feel a slight tingly sensation?

STEP 2: LIGHT IT UP!

Use the alligator clips to attach a piece of copper wire to the penny and another piece of copper wire to the nail. Next, carefully touch both wires to the metal end of a small flashlight bulb. Does the lightbulb light up?

What's going on?

An electric current is created when electrons flow from one electrode to another through a conductor. In this experiment, the penny and the nail both act as electrodes. The copper wire connecting everything is the conductor. The lemon acts to finish the circuit while keeping the two electrodes apart (actually, the juice inside the lemon acts as the conducting fluid, known as the electrolyte). When you put this circuit together, you actually start a chemical reaction in which one of the electrodes loses electrons while the other one gains electrons. That makes the current, which lights up the bulb.

Electrode: something that gives up or accepts electrons to allow electricity to flow.
    Anodes and cathodes are two types of electrodes.

Electrolyte: a substance that will separate into electrically charged parts in solution and become able to conduct electricity.

Electric details

In a battery, to make electrons flow from one electrode to the other, the two electrodes must have different properties. One of them is called the cathode and the other is called the anode. The difference between the cathode and the anode is that the metal at the cathode gains electrons, and the metal at the anode loses electrons. The chemical reactions that occur at each electrode are specialized as well: the reaction at the cathode is called a reduction reaction, whereas the reaction at the anode is called an oxidation reaction. In your lemon battery, the nail is the anode and the penny is the cathode.

The acid in the lemon juice plays a very important role in the success of the battery. The acid is able to react with active metals such as the zinc in the galvanized nail. This reaction causes the zinc to give up electrons; this transfer of electrons is essential for creating electricity.

You may notice small bubbles near the place where the nail is pushed into the lemon. These are bubbles of hydrogen gas, which is produced when hydrogen ions in the lemon juice react with the electrons that were freed from the zinc atoms in the nail.

The future

So, you've finally done it. You've finished all the experiments in this book. You've researched the facts, uncovered each mystery, and you've been careful and thorough—just like a real scientist. So what now?

The information in this book is meant to be a starting point. Use what you've learned to continue experimenting. Did you think of something else you'd like to know? Look it up! Did you think of something else you'd like to try? Design an experiment! The world is your laboratory. Explore away!

Bibliography

Alberts, Bruce, Alexander Johnson, Julian Lewis, Martin Raff, Keith Roberts, and Peter Walters. *Molecular Biology of the Cell*, fourth edition. New York and London: Garland Science, 2002.

Atlas, Ronald M., and Richard Bartha. *Microbial Ecology*, third edition. Redwood City, CA: Benjamin Cummings, 1993.

Bardhan-Quallen, Sudipta. *Last-Minute Science Fair Projects*. New York: Sterling, 2006.

———. *Championship Science Fair Experiments*. New York: Sterling, 2004.

Berg, Jeremy M., John L. Tymoczko, and Lubert Stryer. *Biochemistry*. New York: W. H. Freeman, 2002.

Bottone, Frank G. *The Science of Life: Projects and Principles for Beginning Biologists*. Chicago: Chicago Review Press, 2001.

Deacon, James W. *Fungal Biology*, fourth edition. Malden, MA: Wiley-Blackwell, 2005.

Giancoli, Douglas C. *Physics: Principles with Applications*, sixth edition. Upper Saddle River, NJ: Prentice Hall, 2004.

Halliday, David, Robert Resnick, and Jearl Walker. *Fundamentals of Physics*, seventh edition. Hoboken: Wiley, 2004.

Hudson, Barbara K. *Microbiology in Today's World*, second edition. Dubuque, IA: Kendall-Hunt, 1998.

Lister, Ted, and Heston Blumenthal. *Kitchen Chemistry*. London: Royal Society of Chemistry, 2005.

Madigan, Michael T., John M. Martinko, and Jack Parker. *Brock Biology of Microorganisms*, ninth edition. Upper Saddle River NJ: Prentice Hall, 2000.

Silberberg, Martin S. *Chemistry: The Molecular Nature of Matter and Change*, fifth edition. Boston: McGraw-Hill Science/Engineering/Math, 2008.

Zumdahl, Steven, and Susan Zumdahl. *Chemistry*, seventh edition. Florence, KY: Brooks Cole, 2006.

Photo Credits

Index